Experiments with SOIL

Christine Taylor-Butler

www.raintreepublishers.co.uk
Visit our website to find out more information about Raintree books.

To order:
☎ Phone 0845 6044371
🖹 Fax +44 (0) 1865 312263
🖳 Email myorders@raintreepublishers.co.uk

Customers from outside the UK please telephone +44 1865 312262

Raintree is an imprint of Capstone Global Library Limited, a company incorporated in England and Wales having its registered office at 7 Pilgrim Street, London, EC4V 6LB – Registered company number: 6695582

Text © Capstone Global Library Limited 2011
First published in hardback in 2011
The moral rights of the proprietor have been asserted.

Edited by Rebecca Rissman, Dan Nunn, and Catherine Veitch
Designed by Richard Parker
Picture research by Tracy Cummins
Originated by Capstone Global Library
Printed and bound in China by South China Printing Co. Ltd

ISBN 978 1 406 22909 7
15 14 13 12 11
10 9 8 7 6 5 4 3 2 1

British Library Cataloguing in Publication Data
Taylor-Butler, Christine.
Experiments with soil. -- (My science investigations)
631.4'078-dc22
A full catalogue record for this book is available from the British Library.

Acknowledgements
We would like to thank the following for permission to reproduce photographs: Corbis pp. 6 (© Ocean), 28 (© Didier Dutheil/Sygma); Getty Images pp. 5 (National Geographic/ Carsten Peter), 29 (Noel Hendrickson); Heinemann Raintree pp. 10, 11, 12, 13, 14, 16, 17, 18, 20, 21, 22, 24, 25, 26 (Karon Dubke); istockphoto p. 9 (© SpellbindMe); Shutterstock p. 4, 8 (© psnoonan), 15 (© saiko3p).

Cover photograph of a girl planting seeds reproduced with permission of Getty Images (Garry Wade). Background photograph of a grass and soil background reproduced with permission of Shutterstock (Nina Malyna).

Special thanks to Suzy Gazlay for her invaluable help in the preparation of this book. We would also like to thank Ashley Wolinski for her help in the preparation of this book.

Every effort has been made to contact copyright holders of material reproduced in this book. Any omissions will be rectified in subsequent printings if notice is given to the publisher.

Community Learning & Libraries
Cymuned Ddysgu a Llyfrgelloedd

This item should be returned or renewed by the
last date stamped below.

To renew visit:

www.newport.gov.uk/libraries

Contents

Some words are printed in bold, **like this**.
You can find out what they mean by looking
in the Glossary.

Soil matters

Soil is the top layer of ground that you can grow plants in. It is a mixture of water, air, tiny rocks, and bits of plants and animals.

Geologists are scientists who study Earth and the **materials** from which it is made, including soil. A scientist who studies soil in particular is called a **pedologist**.

How scientists work

Scientists start with a question about something they **observe**, or notice. They gather information and think about it. Then they make a guess, or **hypothesis**, about a likely answer to their question. Next they set up an **experiment** to test their hypothesis. They look at the **data**, or **results**, and make a decision, or a **conclusion,** about whether their hypothesis is right or wrong.

Whether a hypothesis is right or wrong, scientists still learn from each experiment.

How to do an experiment

1. Start a **log**. Write down your **observations**, question, and hypothesis.
2. Plan step by step how you can test the hypothesis. This is called the **procedure**.
3. Carry out the experiment. **Record** everything that happens. These are your observations.
4. Compare your results with your hypothesis. Was your hypothesis right or wrong? What did you learn? The answer is your conclusion.

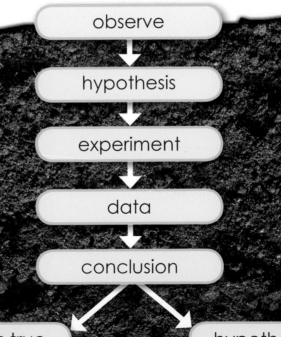

observe

↓

hypothesis

↓

experiment

↓

data

↓

conclusion

hypothesis true   hypothesis false

What's in that soil?

Soil is all around us. It is in gardens and flower beds. It is beneath the pavements and houses. Soil is not exactly the same everywhere. What is the soil made of where you live?

Procedure

1. Dig up a cup of soil. Dig down a little way to get more than just the soil that's on top.

2. Look at the soil carefully. Then, put one spoonful of the soil on a piece of paper. Use a pencil to spread it out. Make a list in your **log** of everything you see.

The science explained

Soil contains plant and animal **material** called **humus**. It may also contain tiny bits of **clay**, **silt**, and **sand**. Clay feels slippery. Silt is gritty and has very small grains. The larger grains are sand. You may also see small rocks and pebbles.

Look carefully at the soil you dig up.

Hypothesis

Soil near plants has more **humus** than soil where no plants are growing.

Procedure

1. Dig up a cup of soil near some plants and fill a jar halfway. Does the soil contain rocks, **sand**, or other objects? What colour is it? What is its **texture**? **Record** your **observations**.

You will need these things for your **experiment**.

2. Add water until the jar is almost full. Replace the lid. Shake the jar, then let the mixture rest for one hour.

3. How many layers do you see? What is in each layer?

4. Find an area where no plants grow. Dig up some soil and repeat steps 1 to 3.

5. Compare the two jars. How are the layers alike? How are they different? Which jar has a thicker layer of humus? Record your observations.

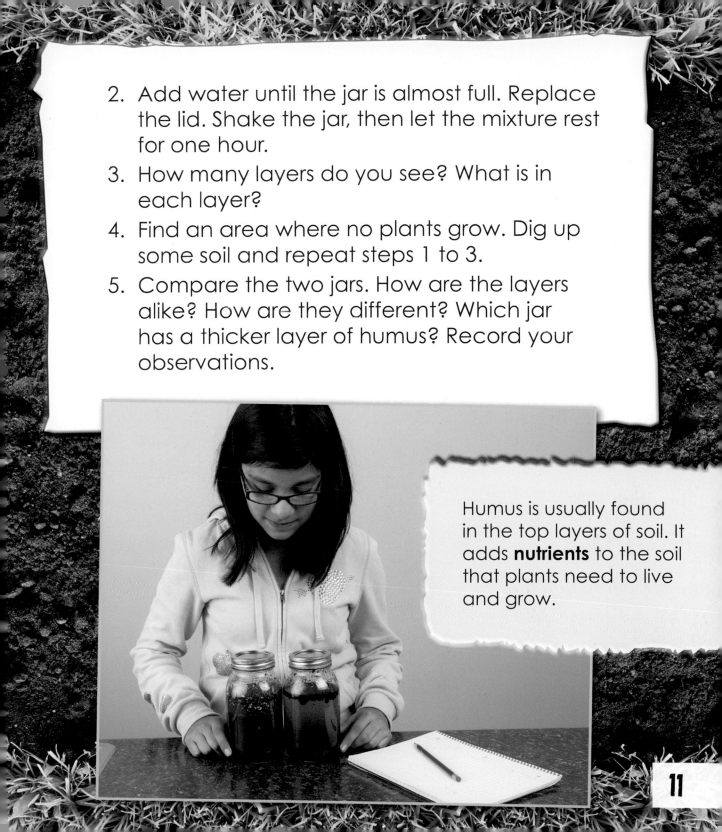

Humus is usually found in the top layers of soil. It adds **nutrients** to the soil that plants need to live and grow.

Hold the water

Plants need the right amount of water to grow. Do all types of soil hold water equally well?

Potting soil has a lot of **humus** and sometimes some **sand** in it. Sandy soil doesn't contain much humus. Garden soil may have some sand in it.

Hypothesis

Sandy soil doesn't hold water as well as soil with less sand and more humus.

Collect these things for the **experiment**. Try to find garden soil, potting soil, and sandy soil.

Procedure

1. Measure one cup of sandy soil into a jar.
2. Measure one cup of water and slowly pour it onto the sandy soil. What do you **observe**?
3. Repeat steps 1 and 2 with garden soil and potting soil. Use a different jar for each soil.
4. Compare what you see in each jar. Which type of soil is **absorbing** the most water?

Record your **observations** in your **log**.

5. Place a small sieve over an empty measuring jug. Pour the sandy soil from the first jar into the sieve. Wait for 10 minutes. How much water came out of the sand? **Record** the **results**.

6. Repeat step 5 with the garden soil and potting soil.

7. Any water that did not come back into the measuring jug is being held by the soil. Which soil held the most water? Which soil held the least water?

You may need to use a spoon to scrape all the soil out of the jar.

The science explained

Plants take in water from soil through their **roots**. Plants cannot have too much water or they will rot. Too little will cause them to dry out. Plants grow best in soil with a mix of sand and **humus**.

Look at this soil. Do you think it contains sand or humus? Or does it contain both?

Clean it up!

The water in natural springs is very clean. How can water from under the ground be clean? The answer is that soil acts as a natural **filter**!

In this **experiment** you will compare four types of soil to see which is the best filter.

Hypothesis

The mixture of **sand**, soil, and rocks will be the best filter.

You will need these things for the experiment.

Procedure

1. Use a toothpick to poke five holes in the bottoms of four paper cups.
2. Fill cup 1 with sand. Fill cup 2 with soil. Fill cup 3 with rocks. Fill cup 4 with equal parts of sand, soil, and rocks .
3. Now make some dirty water. Measure one tablespoon of salt, pepper, spices, and powdered drink mix into four more empty cups.
4. Fill these cups with water and stir well.

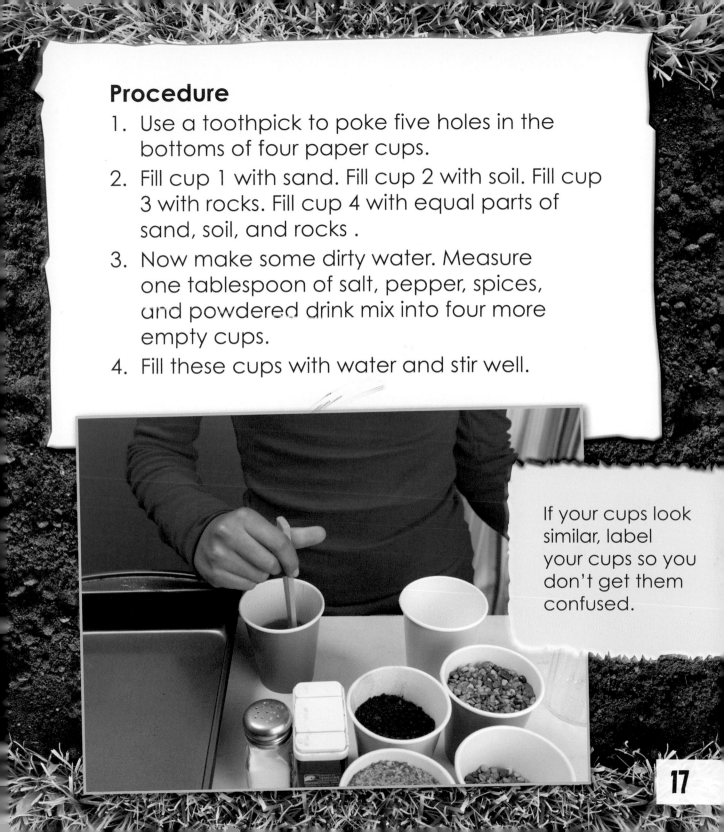

If your cups look similar, label your cups so you don't get them confused.

5. Hold cup 1 over an empty glass. Pour one cup of dirty water into cup 1. Let the water drip into the glass.

6. Repeat step 5 with cups 2, 3, and 4. Each time use a different water glass to catch the dripping water.

7. **Record** your **observations** in your **log**. Which water glass holds the cleanest water? Which soil was the best **filter**? Why do you think so?

Look carefully at the water that drips into the glass.

sand	soil	rocks	mix

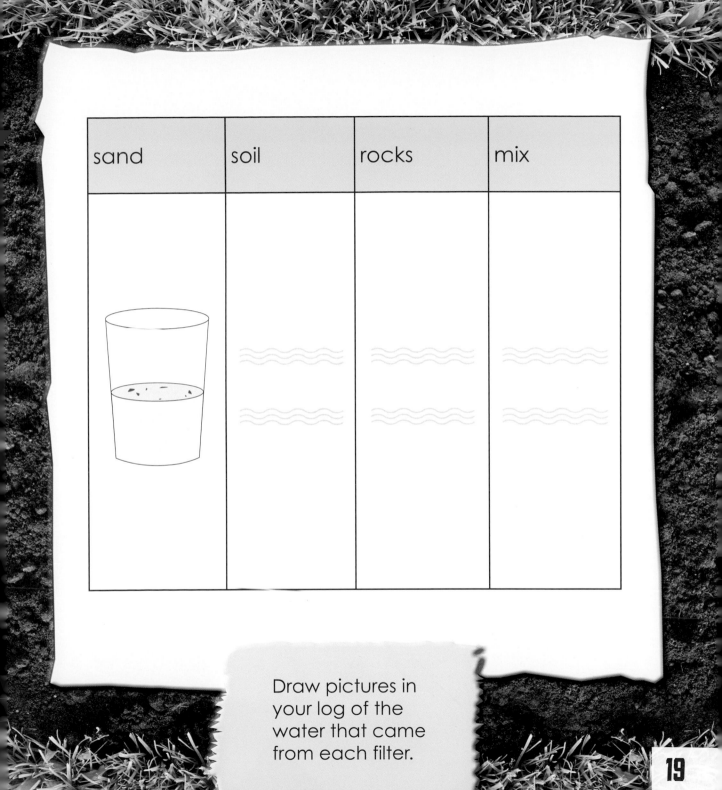

Draw pictures in your log of the water that came from each filter.

Fertilize it!

In order to grow, plants need water, sunlight, and **nutrients**. Good soil contains nutrients, but sometimes there aren't enough or they run out. A gardener can help by adding **fertilizer** so that the plants will grow stronger and faster.

Hypothesis

Plants given fertilizer will grow faster than those without it.

You will need these things for the **experiment**.

Procedure

1. Cover the bottoms of three pots with rocks. Fill them to the top with potting soil. Label the pots fertilizer 1, fertilizer 2, and **control**.

2. Press one teaspoon of seeds into each pot.

3. Add one teaspoon of fertilizer to fertilizer 1 pot. Do the same to fertilizer 2 pot.

4. Add water to all three pots until moist.

Labelling your pots will help you remember which is which.

5. Put the pots where all three get the same amount of sunlight and heat.
6. **Observe** the pots every morning for two weeks. **Record** your **observations**.

The soil in the middle pot is a **control**. Nothing has been added to it. Scientists use a control to compare what happens when they change something. The change was adding **fertilizer** to the other two pots.

Using a control helps you to see how much more your plants grow with fertilizer.

7. Compare your **results** for all three pots.
   Did the fertilizer help the seeds to grow?

	Fertilizer 1 pot	Control	Fertilizer 2 pot
Description of plant after one week			
Description of plant after two weeks			

Record your findings in a table like this in your **log**.

Now you see it

What happens when the **nutrients** in the soil are used up? Nature replaces nutrients in the soil. Insects, earthworms, bacteria, and other **decomposers** break down dead plants and animal parts to form **compost**. In time, compost becomes part of the soil.

Hypothesis

Compost forms more quickly in the light than in the dark.

You will need these things for the **experiment**.

Procedure

1. Make layers 2 centimetres deep of soil, grass, leaves, and fruit or vegetable scraps in a glass jar. Sprinkle two tablespoons of water between each layer.

2. Cover with soil. Add 3 tablespoons of water, or until moist. Draw a picture of your compost.

You can also add strips of old paper to your jar.

3. Place the jar on a sunny window ledge.
4. Repeat steps 1-3. Make the jars as similar as possible. Place the second jar in a very dark place, such as a cupboard.
5. **Observe** the jars every day for a week. Use a magnifying glass to get a closer look. Write your **observations** in your **log**. When does the **material** start to break up, or **decay**?

Look in your jars to see if the layers are decaying.

The science explained

The **compost** you made is full of **nutrients**. Nutrients help things grow. Many plants grow well in composted soil.

How have the mixtures changed? Draw pictures in your log to help you keep track.

Your turn!

Scientists study soil to find out more about the world's history. They study soil to solve crimes. They even study soil from other planets, such as Mars, to learn more about the planet. Scientists also study soil to find new ways to feed people.

Soil helps plants grow. Some scientists are trying to find ways to grow plants without soil. Do you think it's possible? How can you find out? Design an **experiment** to see if you can grow healthy plants without soil.

Glossary

absorb suck up, or take in

clay fine-grained, slippery material in soil

compost decomposed material that provides nutrients in soil for plants

conclusion what you learn from the results of an experiment

control part of an experiment where nothing is changed

data information gathered in an experiment

decay break down or rot

decomposers organisms that break down plant and animal material

experiment organized way of testing an idea

fertilizer something added to soil to help plants grow

filter remove dirt or other solids

geologist scientist who studies rocks and soil

humus plant and animal matter in soil

hypothesis suggested statement or explanation that can be tested

log written notes about an experiment

material what something is made out of

nutrient food, nourishment

observation something that you notice using any of your five senses

observe watch, or notice something

pedologist scientist who studies soil

procedure steps followed to carry out an experiment

record draw or write something down

results what happens in an experiment

roots underground part of a plant. Plants take in water from the soil through their roots.

sand small, loose grains of rock

silt small-grained, gritty material in soil

texture how something feels when you touch it. For example, smooth or rough.

Find out more

Books

Plants: Roots. Patricia Whitehouse, (Raintree, 2009)

Soil (Let's Rock), Louise Spilsbury and Richard Spilsbury (Raintree, 2011)

Super Cool Science Experiments: Soil (Science Explorer), Vicky Franchino (Cherry Lake, 2009)

Websites

www.bbc.co.uk/schools/ks2bitesize/ science/materials/rocks_soils/read1.shtml
Visit this website to learn about rocks and soils, including a fun game and a quiz.

www.channel4learning.com/apps26/learning/ microsites/E/essentials/science/ material/rockssoils_bi.jsp
Learn about rocks and soils, with activities, key terms, and more on this website.

Index